Song Mamma

Stories of Connecting through Song

Pip Cooper

Photography by
Andy Toohey

Balboa Press books may be ordered through booksellers or by contacting:

Balboa Press
A Division of Hay House
1663 Liberty Drive
Bloomington, IN 47403
www.balboapress.com.au
1 (877) 407-4847

Because of the dynamic nature of the Internet, any web addresses or links contained in this book may have changed since publication and may no longer be valid. The views expressed in this work are solely those of the author and do not necessarily reflect the views of the publisher, and the publisher hereby disclaims any responsibility for them.

Interior Image Credit: Andy Toohey

ISBN: 978-1-5043-1968-3 (sc)
ISBN: 978-1-5043-1969-0 (e)

Print information available on the last page.

Balboa Press rev. date: 11/15/2019

Introduction

The idea for Song Mamma came to me when I recorded a CD of songs for my two older children. I was seven months pregnant with my youngest child at the time and was doing a 40-minute "performance" each evening as my children went to bed. It was exhausting! However, I wanted my children to continue to hear my voice and enjoy the songs I had sung to them since they were in utero.

I had never recorded my singing voice before and even though a friend was doing the recording, I was as nervous as hell. My voice reflected that—shaky, weak and emotion-filled. My kids, however, seemed to notice none of this! They enthusiastically played my singing wherever we went, no matter who the audience, which was somewhat embarrassing for me. I continued to sing to them and with them, but I no longer did the 40-minute performances each evening. As my pregnancy progressed, I was grateful for that.

When my children were able to have their own rooms, I had the pleasure of hearing myself in stereo whenever they felt like listening to me sing. Again, this was a little unnerving and I always wished they would turn it off when people came to visit, but they never did. They loved "Mummy's Songs" and proudly played them.

I came to understand from this experience that while I may think my voice is not worthy of praise (and endlessly being listened to), my kids think it is, and they find comfort and connection through my voice. It makes sense really; my voice is the first one they ever heard, and children seem to equate this with comfort, warmth, and nourishment. I sang to them as babies, as toddlers, and as small children, and now I sing with them as older children. They know the words to all the songs I sang over the years and often request their favourites. Some of them are kids' songs, but many are not. I change the volume, tone and speed of the song depending on what the situation requires—are they after soothing and comfort, or a bit of a musical romp?

Many parents told me what a lovely idea it was, to have recorded songs for my kids. However, many also never sang to their children because, as they said, "I can't sing!" and—echoing my own thoughts—"I can't remember any songs; I only know the chorus." That's why on this CD you'll hear kids' songs, grown-up songs and made-up songs—songs that have been changed a bit and personalized. It really doesn't matter what you sing or what you think your singing voice is like, your kids will respond to it. Your voice is a gift to you and your children; you have it with you 24/7 and in every situation; it is there for you to comfort, soothe, connect with or play with your child, and best of all it's FREE.

Something else I hear a lot is, "My kids tell me to stop singing when I do it," the implication being, "They don't like my voice because I sound awful or it's embarrassing to them." My thoughts on this are to look within yourself; are they merely reflecting back to you what you really think of your singing voice? Is it *you* who thinks it's awful and embarrassing to hear you sing? And is there a part of you that gets a lot of pleasure from singing anyway? If the answer is yes to these questions, then I would encourage you to keep singing regardless; focus on the pleasure you get from singing and ignore that critical voice saying to stop. There is great healing in expressing your voice freely, and while this is not my area of expertise, healing through song has definitely been part of my journey.

As I've described my vision of Song Mamma to others and how this process has evolved, I've been asked by a few people to share the story of Song Mamma's unfolding: the time it's taken, the ebbs and flows along the way, the doubts, the highs, and finally this wonderful end result.

In truth, this project has taken me more than nine years to bring to fruition. In that time I've moved house, renovated said house, taken my two oldest children out of school to homeschool/unschool them, gone back to my healing work, facilitated Mothers' retreats, and so much more. However, the major reason this project has taken so long to come together is that I've simply followed the energy of the project. When things are fired up and energized, a great boost in activity has taken place—the recording done, the photos taken, or the stories collated. As a busy Mum, I have deliberately tried not to stress about this wonderful project happening, rather, I have just trusted it will happen as and when it is meant to. In doing this, I have noticed how easily everything has come together, and the amount of support that has been available to me is incredible. All this has created a project that has not been stressful, awkward or at any point boring. This is grassroots project which has come together with virtually no money; much of what has been achieved has been done via bartering and exchange. This has worked for all involved and leaves me with a feeling of great love and support because, to be honest, if I'd had to find the money to make this happen I'm not sure it ever would have.

The overwhelming feeling of this project is joy; whenever I have worked with anyone on this it has been a great deal of fun, and there has been immense respect and care between all of us as we work. The Mums have given their time freely as I have worked to fit into their crazy and ever-changing schedules. Recording the songs and doing the photo shoot were such organic processes—with babes in arms, me caring for children as their Mums recorded inside, ordering another coffee for our photographer or for one of the Mums as her photo was being taken. Whatever we've done, it has been cooperative and easy. Much of what has happened has been a new experience, not only for me but for the Mums, the photographer, the artist, and the recording engineer. Whether it's having our voices recorded for the first time, having a professional photo taken of ourselves, working in exchange for services rather than cash, having freedom of creative expression, or not working to a rigid deadline, all this has been part of the project and we have all enjoyed playing our part in its creation. Almost everyone has told me how privileged they feel to have been asked to work on Song Mamma, and I feel privileged to have had them agree to it! This has been a new way of working for me—I must say I really like it and I will endeavour to emulate it in future projects.

There were times, I have to admit, when I didn't think the project would ever get off the ground or be finished, but I decided to trust the process and just follow the prompts as they came to me. Thus as I now head into the ninth year of working on this, I know it will be completed. It will be a vastly different project to the one I set out to create, but a better one for the time and love it has taken to bring it to you.

To access songs please use the link *www.songmamma.com/songs/*

My Mamma Songs are Morningtown Ride (The Seekers) *and* My Favourite Things (Rogers & Hammerstein).

I sang *Morningtown Ride* (The Seekers) mostly at bedtime to both my daughters. I think they particularly liked the rhythm and sang along with the chorus. *My Favourite Things* (Rogers & Hammerstein) probably started with my older daughter, Jasmine (now 28), watching *The Sound of Music* with my mother—her grandma. I particularly sang this song to the girls when they were sad or upset at bedtime, or finding it hard to get sleep. Jasmine would also sing it to her half-sister, Rose (14 years her junior), when she was younger and still lived at home with us.

Helen Archer

My Mamma Song is Heidi Heidi Ho (public domain).

My Lily found it difficult to let go and relax, as she was (and still is) wired for action, not relaxing. So between us, we had a long process of sleepless nights to see what would assist her body to let go and go to sleep.

A good friend gave us a tape of slow-down songs, which had *Heidi Heidi Ho* (public domain) on it. She didn't respond to the song on tape, but when I began to sing it without the tape, she sighed and listened as I rocked her side to side, like a big slow elephant.

Hooray! We found the song that worked. As she got older, the song still worked, but we imagined her on the animal's back—that way, she could visualise with the song, going for a ride.

Now she sings it to me sometimes and she still relaxes…and I have fallen to sleep. Forever our song.

Kerri-Anne Brogan

My Mamma Songs are The Nonsense Song *(my made-up name because I have no idea what it's called!) and* Donna (Joan Baez).

Friends surprised me with a guitar for my 21ˢᵗ birthday. I took it with me when I set out travelling and collected songs over the next almost three years, as I journeyed through Asia, India and the Middle East. I can't remember where I learned these songs, who from, or what they're actually called, but they were colourful threads in the rich fabric of that time of my life.

When I had children I would sometimes sing *Donna* (Joan Baez) to my three sons at bedtime as a lullaby. It is very soothing while talking about the difficulty of life, and inspires a wish, to fly above it all. Very helpful to me when, as Mothers do, I was stressing!!

The Nonsense song is just a bit of fun that bubbles up anytime day or night, cooking, walking, in the car—wherever.

Francine Bartlett

My Mamma Song is All the Pretty Little Horses (public domain).

I think many things were in my head when I would sing this to my son Marcus as a lullaby to put him to sleep. My nephew Joshua would also always ask for it if I was babysitting him—he'd have remembered it from shared bedtimes at either my or his place. For Marcus it was my way of including his father who I had separated from—I think it's the strong masculinity in the images of horses

Marilyn Gottlieb

My Mamma Songs are Mockingbird Song (Inez Foxx) *and* Princess (Cindy original).

I sang the *Mockingbird Song* (Inez Foxx) in a play when I was in high school, many, many moons ago. I was playing a young mother contemplating what my child would grow up to be. The song stayed with me throughout my teens, twenties and into my thirties, when I was lucky enough to have two little babies of my own. I would sing this song, in my sleep if necessary, and it would always soothe the anxieties away from my little ones (and myself).

Once the girls were older I used to tell them stories or read a book before bed. One evening, the girls requested a song "from my head". I just started singing and out *Princess* (Cindy original) popped. The favourite part is the ending when we all add everybody we can possibly think of who we love. The list became quite long when they started pre-school, then swimming lessons, etc, etc! At the end of the song the girls would usually end up laughing and be more awake than when I started, so I would have to sing a different song!

Now the girls are in their teens and experiencing high school and all the hormones that go with this stage of life. They don't request songs or stories like they used to, but every now and again, when I feel like they are drifting away, I sing and we are close for a pinch of a moment more. And I'm left wondering…what are my babies going to be when they grow up?

Cindy Pryma

My Mamma Songs are My Pigeon House (public domain) *and* Bluebells, Cockle Shells (public domain).

Five daughters, six grandchildren and thirty years of evolving and running Playsessions at North Sydney Leisure (now Community) Centre and eventually, Crow's Nest T.A.F.E College Child Care Course, have left me with a great respect for creative play—music, painting and collage, books, puzzles, water play, and sensory experiences using colour, goop, slime, frothy water etc. Sound like Pre-school? Not quite. With attending Mothers, sometimes Dads, or Nannies, Playsessions were unstructured but supervised opportunities for children to play and explore! It also gave the adults an understanding of the value of play—social, cognitive, manipulative and creative.

All these years, with encouragement and mentoring from many others, left me with a huge repertoire of songs, many my own—active and passive, loud and quiet, rocking and gentle, sitting and standing, clapping, jumping, swaying and eventually joining hands for a circle song. All were involved, and it was great fun.

Hopefully, Playsession Music enriched the repertoire of the often enormous number of participants (many of whom traveled long distances to attend), encouraged confidence in the adult non-singers, and enhanced the language and listening skills in the small enthusiasts. It often involved some improvisation on my part too ("Do you know a song about a scorpion?")!

As for my Mamma Songs, *My Pigeon House* (public domain) was Granddaughter Indianna's 'going to sleep' favourite. I sang it to her…slowly, quietly, sometimes repetitively…till its soporific effect worked its magic.

Bluebells, Cockle Shells (public domain) is a traditional English song, used as a lullaby. This song was *'caught'*—to use my mentor, Dr. Doreen (Dee) Bridge's term, as she said children *'catch'* songs—when my youngest daughter Camilla and I were lucky enough to attend the Early Music Classes Dee offered in Sydney in 1981. It has been part of most Playsession Music since. Perfect for gently rocking babies…and with a small surprise to finish!

Jan Gregg

My Mamma Song is Aa aa allin lasta (public domain)—*a traditional Finnish lullaby.*

The tune of *Aa aa allin lasta* (public domain) is typically Finnish—monotonous and repetitive, and in a minor key. In fact, several other Finnish lullabies I know of have a very similar tune. The words are about an orphaned little waterbird "with no father, or a mother to take care of the little one". But that's just the first verse; the second is sung to the child, and the last line is much more assuring: "there is a father, there is a mother, to take care of the little one".

I think I used Elsie's name in the second verse and varied the tune a bit. I sang this to Elsie when she was quite small, as a soothing song, and I've sung it recently only when she has been a bit poorly.

Anni Heino

My Mamma Songs are Skye Boat Song (Sir Harold Boulton/Robert Louis Stevenson), Nighty Night Sleepy Tight (Brahms Lullaby – Johannes Brahms) *and* Stout Little Cup (Julie original).

Skye Boat Song (Sir Harold Boulton/Robert Louis Stevenson) was on a record my Mum and Dad had when I was a little girl. I loved the lilting female voice and the beautiful imagery of a boat sailing across the oceans carrying a little boy "born to be king". I sang this to both my children, but particularly Joshua, as I loved imagining the idea that he too was "born to be king" or some other form of greatness. I found it soothing for both of us.

"Nighty night Sleepy Tight" is *Brahms Lullaby* (Johannes Brahms), which was sung to me by my Dad in German when I was small. The words are a mish-mash of things that Dave and I came up with and started singing every night to Hannah when she was a baby. It simply became the cue for all of us to quieten down and prepare for sleep. She loved it too as she could make up her own words to it once she could speak; it often became quite funny or ridiculous. Josh has been put to sleep with it too, so it is now simply one of our family classics.

Stout Little Cup is an original I came up with in my twenties and wanted to share with my kids, as it was a side of me that they hadn't really seen. They laugh hysterically and try to copy the voice that I do and it's really just a bit of fun that we all share.

Julie Wood

My Mamma Songs are K.i.s.s.i.n.g (public domain) and I can sing a Rainbow (Arthur Hamilton)

We like these songs as they are easy and we can just sing them over and over. Singing brings us together in the car.

Kylie Woods

My Mamma Song is my own interpretation of Didn't Leave Nobody But the Baby (Emmy Lou Harris).

My mother sang to my sisters and me as children, so it was only natural I should sing to my child. Having worked as a singer before I became pregnant, I was accustomed to expressing myself through song. I remember lying awake at night with my unborn baby tap-dancing across my belly in the wee small hours, thinking about all the possibilities of being on my own with her when I could at last see her face to kiss it…so I just sang. I sang to invite calm for us both.

After Indianna was born, this song came back to me one summer evening, once the song of the cicadas had quietened. My girl's tired eyes were resisting sleep, so I let my own version of the song flow without constraint. I had always felt a connection to this piece. The melody is soporific and the lyrics not only aim to hush the restless child but also speak of love, strength, loneliness and redemption. She was my world now and this folk song became my affirmation that I was strong enough to overcome anything that tried to disempower our relationship.

My baby girl is now a teenager yet she still remembers me singing this song to lull her to sleep. Although we often sing together, like a ribbon that ties us, Indi really loves singing for herself now. Her voice is a big part of her identity. As for 'going to sleep'? Her night owl status remains. But she will often go to bed listening to the songs that welcome rest.

Rachel Gregg

My Mamma Songs are Hashi Venu (public domain), Shima (public domain), Baa Baa Black Sheep (public domain) *and* Noyana (public domain).

Shima (public domain) is my daughter Malaika's favourite of the songs I sing and she frequently requests it when I am settling her or needing to soothe her—either to sleep or just for comfort. I have sung this song over the phone and via Skype when she has been away and the distance too great for me to pick her up. It is almost miraculous how it soothes her and those listening in the background. It's a strong and beautiful connection to my girl.

Baa Baa Black Sheep (public domain) is the silly song that has been a favourite for each of my kids. I originally sang it in French because I was bored with singing it in English over and over to my eldest child, Steel. I remembered learning the song in my French class at school many years ago and decided I'd give it a try in French. Unfortunately, I couldn't remember all the words and was actually unsure the words were correct. I found that funny so did it anyway, and wouldn't you know it, Steel loved it too! He often requested I sing the French version as bad as I thought it was. It then became an oft-requested song from my other kids too, so I've been singing this silly version for over a decade.

Pip Cooper

Noyana (public domain) is Amelie's song of choice and her request for this CD. It is a gentle, lulling song and she loves songs sung in other languages. Of all my children she is the one who will settle almost as soon as I open my mouth to sing or she will join in if it's a fun and lively song. It's not surprising really, as I sang all through my pregnancy with her and she was sung into the world by her Dad, midwives and a dear friend.

Hashi Venu (public domain) has been recorded sung as a round with Ganga and Sorcha, with whom I've sung this song a great deal. I chose this Mamma Song because we all sang it as an impromptu round on a rainy car trip to Canberra to attend the Homebirth Rally. My youngest, Amelie, was getting fretful in the back of the car and there was nowhere safe for me to pull over and swap drivers. I began to sing *Hashi Venu* (public domain), one of her favourites, to soothe her. Ganga and Sorcha just joined in. It was a magic moment, which Amelie obviously enjoyed as she quickly settled. This has stayed in mind as one of the most beautiful moments singing for my babe.

My Mamma Songs are Go to Sleep My Darling (public domain) *and* Butterfly (Gail original).

My Grandmother, Agnes Flynn, sang *Go to Sleep My Darling (*public domain*)* to my father when he was a little lad. They were a working class family in the north of England. Agnes was of Irish descent and the song is too. This song was traditionally sung by members of her family to all the little ones to calm them when they were being settled for the evening. My Dad, Anthony, taught me the song.

My husband (also Anthony) and I sing this to our girls, Willow and Arwen every night before bed. They will not go to bed until we sing it to them. It is a lovely tradition to carry through and makes me feel close to my Grandma who passed away when I was a baby. For the lyric, "It's time for little darling baby to say good night", we sing our child's name instead—for example, "It's time for little darling Willow to say good night". They always loved the song being personalised since they were very little. As far as I know, this part of the tradition is particular to my immediate family.

Butterfly was composed by me when Willow was a newborn—17 years ago! I always loved butterflies and my girls do too. She was not easy to settle as a baby, so singing to her helped both of us calm down. Musically, I tried to make it sound like the flittery, fluttery flight of a butterfly. As Willow became a toddler, I added butterfly hand movements which amused her. Sometimes we would sing this at night or to distract her when she was upset. Although we don't sing it as much now that my girls are older, 16 and 18, they remember it fondly and smile and join in now.

Gail Waizer

My Mamma Songs are The Darling Song (Suo Gan – Welsh Traditional) *and* We'll be Together (Ganga original).

The Darling Song (public domain)

When our daughter was a baby, she suffered from Gastro Intestinal Reflux and found settling and sleep difficult, as she was often in pain.

Something that gave her comfort was when I sang to her. Apart from toning single notes and hours of harmonic overtoning, I wanted (mainly for my own sanity) to sing an actual song.

I had learned the beautiful Welsh lullaby *Suo Gân* (public domain)in English when I was conducting the NSW Primary Choral Concerts at the Sydney Opera House. However, I found that singing the same two verses to a distressed baby for that length of time became a bit monotonous, so I started to improvise. I found myself recounting the events and activities of the day, always with the focus on how exhausting it all must have been and that sleep would be the obvious solution. When she was a toddler, Acacia began to ask for this song that always began with "Sleep my Darling…". So, her own personalised song about her day was born and she still refers to it as "The Darling Song" (public domain).

*We'll be Together (*Ganga original*)*

When our son was a baby, his sleep song was the mantra Om Gam Ganapatayei Namaha—for removing obstacles—to sleep! Realising as a toddler that his sister had a bedtime song of her own he (quite understandably) wanted a song that was just for him.

Based loosely on the chorus of Leonard Cohen's *Hallelujah*, my husband Anthony wrote him this song that Rowan still, at age eight, sings along with each of us every night (including the ridiculously high note at the end!), complete with actions.

It's so delicious to sing together and it delineates bedtime clearly, gently and nurtures us all.

Ganga Karen Ashworth

My Mamma Songs are Holy Shla Shla (public domain), and Full flaming fire (Waldorf songs).

There are two girls who hold a special place in my heart, held for them alone. As my role in their life has evolved and deepened, from step-mumma to auntie or friend, the essential love, trust and deep familiarity hasn't changed. Singing to my Lamber and Isis as they settled into peaceful slumber, or through distress and sickness, has been one of the deep joys of my life.

Through this blessing I have learnt that with children, one can be utterly unselfconscious in singing, allowing the cracks and squeaks to emerge (as they inevitably will at that time of night). They don't hear them. They seem to hear only your pure intention.

When I sing to the girls, I always imagine that my voice is like a blanket: it soothes, connects, nurtures and embraces. It wraps around them and they have my unconditional presence, where essentially they feel loved and valued, warm and supported. My heart connects to theirs. Often too, we would sing our songs joyfully together.

The songs chosen were, at the time of recording, their individual favourites—songs that in my mind belonged, for that moment, only to them. They were utterly delighted that 'their' songs would be on a CD!

The process of recording was a special one in itself. The 'right' take was absolutely the one where I allowed my eyes to close; I imagined their little bodies in my arms, and felt that indescribable feeling of heart connection arise. As tears emerged, we had the one! My voice had simply sung itself!

I am so blessed to be part of this beautiful project as an honorary mumma, of sorts. And I thank Pip for her dedication, friendship and love. Most importantly I send Sorchie love and hugs to 'holy shla shla mylamby loo, and the ever keen 'just one more, Sorchie' Izzy woo.

Sorcha Conlan

Printed in the United States
By Bookmasters